TURNING GOALS INTO
RESULTS

HARVARD BUSINESS REVIEW
CLASSICS

TURNING GOALS INTO RESULTS

The Power of Catalytic Mechanisms

Jim Collins

Harvard Business Review Press
Boston, Massachusetts

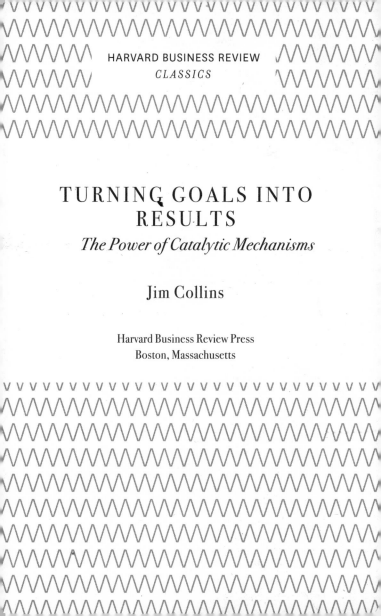

HBR Press Quantity Sales Discounts

Harvard Business Review Press titles are available at significant quantity discounts when purchased in bulk for client gifts, sales promotions, and premiums. Special editions, including books with corporate logos, customized covers, and letters from the company or CEO printed in the front matter, as well as excerpts of existing books, can also be created in large quantities for special needs.

For details and discount information for both print and ebook formats, contact booksales@harvardbusiness.org, tel. 800-988-0886, or www.hbr.org/bulksales.

Copyright 2017 Harvard Business School Publishing Corporation
Originally published in *Harvard Business Review* in July–August 1999
Reprint #3960
All rights reserved

Printed in the United States of America

10 9 8 7 6 5 4 3 2 1

The web addresses referenced in this book were live and correct at the time of the book's publication but may be subject to change.

Library of Congress Cataloging-in-Publication Data
Names: Collins, James C. (James Charles), 1958– author.
Title: Turning goals into results : the power of catalytic mechanisms / Jim Collins.
Other titles: Harvard business review classics.
Description: Boston, Massachusetts : Harvard Business Review Press, [2017] | Series: Harvard Business Review classics
Identifiers: LCCN 2016041613 | ISBN 9781633692589 (pbk.)
Subjects: LCSH: Strategic planning. | Success in business. | Bureaucracy. | Organizational change.
Classification: LCC HD30.28 .C64317 2017 | DDC 658.4/012–dc23 LC record available at https://lccn.loc.gov/2016041613

ISBN: 978-1-63369-258-9
eISBN: 978-1-63369-259-6

THE HARVARD BUSINESS
REVIEW CLASSICS SERIES

Since 1922, *Harvard Business Review* has been a leading source of breakthrough ideas in management practice—many of which still speak to and influence us today. The HBR Classics series now offers you the opportunity to make these seminal pieces a part of your permanent management library. Each volume contains a groundbreaking idea that has shaped best practices and inspired countless managers around the world—and will change how you think about the business world today.

TURNING GOALS INTO RESULTS

Most executives have a big, hairy, audacious goal. One dreams of making his brand more popular than Coke; another aspires to create the most lucrative Web site in cyberspace; yet another longs to see her organization act with the guts necessary to depose its arch rival. So, too, most executives ardently hope that their outsized goals will become a reality. To that end, they write vision statements, deliver speeches, and launch change initiatives. They devise complicated incentive programs, formalize rules and checklists, and pen policies and procedures. In other words, with the best intentions, they create layer upon layer of stultifying bureaucracy. Is it any surprise that their wildly ambitious dreams are seldom realized?

But companies don't have to act that way. Over the past six years, I have observed and studied a simple yet extremely powerful managerial tool that helps organizations turn goals into results. I have recently codified it; I call it the *catalytic mechanism.* Catalytic mechanisms are the crucial link between objectives and performance; they are a galvanizing, nonbureaucratic means to turn one into the other. Put another way, catalytic mechanisms are to visions what the central elements of the U.S. Constitution are to the Declaration of Independence—devices that translate lofty aspirations into concrete reality. They make big, hairy, audacious goals reachable.

My research indicates that few companies—perhaps only 5% or 10%—currently employ catalytic mechanisms, and some of them aren't even aware that they do. I have also found that catalytic mechanisms are relatively easy to create and implement. Given their effectiveness, they are perhaps the most underutilized—and most promising—devices that executives can use to achieve their big, hairy, audacious goals, or BHAGs. (For more on BHAGs, see the box "Anatomy of a BHAG.")

Consider Granite Rock, a 99-year-old company in Watsonville, California, that sells crushed gravel, concrete, sand, and asphalt. Twelve years ago, when brothers Bruce and Steve Woolpert became copresidents, they gave their company a new BHAG. Granite Rock would provide total customer satisfaction and achieve a reputation for service that met or exceeded that of Nordstrom, the upscale department store that is world famous for delighting its customers. Not exactly a timid goal for a stodgy, family-owned company whose employees are mostly tough, sweaty people operating rock quarries and whose customers—mainly tough, sweaty construction workers and contractors—are not easily dazzled.

Now stop and think for a minute: What would it take to actually reach such an ambitious goal? Most people automatically think of galvanizing leadership. But that wasn't an option for Granite Rock, as the Woolperts are a quiet, thoughtful, and bookish clan. Nor did the answer lie in hosting hoopla events or launching grand customer service initiatives. The brothers had seen such efforts at other companies and believed they had little lasting effect.

They chose instead to implement a radical new policy called "short pay." The bottom of every Granite Rock invoice reads, "If you are not satisfied for any reason, don't pay us for it. Simply scratch out the line item, write a brief note about the problem, and return

a copy of this invoice along with your check
for the balance."

Let me be clear about short pay. It is not
a refund policy. Customers do not need to
return the product. They do not need to call
and complain. They have complete discretionary power to decide whether and how
much to pay based on their satisfaction level.

To put the radical nature of short pay
in perspective, imagine paying for airline
tickets after the flight and having the power
to short pay depending on your travel
experience—not just in the air, but during
ticketing and deplaning as well. Or suppose
universities issued tuition invoices at the end
of the semester, along with the statement, "If
you are not satisfied with the dedication of

the professor in any course, simply scratch out that course and send us a tuition check for the balance." Or suppose your cell phone bill came with a statement that said, "If you are not satisfied with the quality of connection of any calls, simply identify and deduct those from the total and send a check for the balance."

In the years since it was instituted, short pay has had a profound and positive impact on Granite Rock. It serves as a warning system, providing hard-to-ignore feedback about the quality of service and products. It impels managers to relentlessly track down the root causes of problems in order to prevent repeated short payments. It signals to employees and customers alike that Granite

Rock is dead serious about customer satisfaction in a way that goes far beyond slogans. Finally, it keeps Granite Rock from basking in the glory of its remarkable success.

And it has had success, as has been widely reported. The little company—it has only 610 employees—has consistently gained market share in a commodity business dominated by behemoths, all the while charging a 6% price premium. It won the prestigious Malcolm Baldrige National Quality Award in 1992. And its financial performance has significantly improved—from razor-thin margins to profit ratios that rival companies like Hewlett-Packard, which has a pretax return of roughly 10%. No doubt, short pay was a critical device for turning the Woolpert brothers' BHAG into a reality.

FIVE PARTS OF A WHOLE

Obviously, not every company should institute short pay. Rather, companies should have catalytic mechanisms as powerful as short pay. What, then, is the difference between a catalytic mechanism and most traditional managerial devices, such as a company's hiring and compensation policies? Catalytic mechanisms share five distinct characteristics. (See the table "Catalytic mechanisms: Breaking from tradition.") Let's look at them in turn.

Characteristic 1: A catalytic mechanism produces desired results in unpredictable ways

When executives identify a bold organizational goal, the first thing they usually do is design a plethora of systems, controls, procedures, and practices that seem likely to make it happen. That process is called alignment, and it's wildly popular in the world of management, among business academics and executives alike. After all, alignment makes sense. If you want to make your brand more popular than Coke, you had better measure the effectiveness of advertising and reward successful marketing managers with big bonuses. But the problem, as I've said, is that the controls that undergird alignment also create bureaucracy, and it should be news to no one that bureaucracy does not breed extraordinary results.

Don't get me wrong. Bureaucracy may deliver results, but they will be mediocre because bureaucracy leads to predictability and conformity. History shows us that organizations achieve greatness when people are allowed to do unexpected things—to show initiative and creativity, to step outside the scripted path. That is when delightful, interesting, and amazing results occur.

Take 3M. For decades, its executives have dreamed of having a constant flow of terrific new products. To achieve that end, in 1956, the company instituted a catalytic mechanism that is by now well known: scientists are urged to spend 15% of their time experimenting and inventing in the area of their own choice. How very unbureaucratic! No one is told what products to work on, just how much to work. And that loosening of controls has led to a stream of profitable innovations, from the famous Post-it Notes to less well-known examples such as reflective license plates and machines that replace the functions of the human heart during surgery. 3M's sales and earnings have increased more than 40-fold since instituting the 15% rule. The mechanism has helped gen-erate cumulative stock returns 36% in excess of the market and has earned the company a frequent ranking in the top ten of *Fortune*'s most-admired list.

In a happy coincidence, the variation sparked by catalytic mechanisms forces learning to occur. Suppose you set out to climb the 3,000-foot sheer rock face of El Capitan in Yosemite Valley. Once you pass pitch 15, you cannot possibly retreat from your particular route: you are, by dint of nature, 100% committed. Although you can't predict *how* you will overcome the remaining pitches—you have to improvise as you go—you can predict that you will invent a way to the top. Why? Because the reality of having no easy retreat forces you to reach the summit. Catalytic mechanisms have the same effect. Granite Rock's short pay commits the company to achieving complete customer satisfaction. Every time a customer exercises short pay, Granite Rock learns or invents a way to run its operations more effectively. Ultimately, such new knowledge leads to better results, making the catalytic mechanism part of a virtuous circle of variation, learning, improvement, and enhanced results.

My "red flag" device also illustrates that circle. When I first began teaching Stanford M.B.A. students by the case method in 1988, I noticed that a small number of them tended to dominate the discussion. I also noticed that there was no correlation between the degree of vocal aggressiveness and how much these students improved the class's overall learning experience. Some vocal students had much to contribute; others just liked to hear themselves talk. Worse, I noticed when chatting with students after class that some of the quieter individuals had significant contributions but were selective or shy about sharing them. Furthermore, seeing 15 to 20 hands raised at a time, I had no way of knowing which one represented a truly significant insight, and I sensed that I was frequently missing some students' one best contribution for the entire quarter.

I solved that problem by giving each student an 8.5 inch by 11 inch bright red sheet of paper at the beginning of every quarter. It had the following instructions: "This is your red flag for the quarter. If you raise your hand with your red flag, the classroom will stop for you. There are no restrictions on when and how to use your red flag; the decision rests entirely in your hands. You can use it to voice an observation, share a personal experience, present an analysis, disagree with the professor, challenge a CEO guest, respond to a fellow student, ask a question, make a suggestion, or whatever. There will be no penalty whatsoever for any use of a red flag. Your red flag can be used only once during the quarter. Your red flag is nontransferable; you cannot give or sell it to another student."

I had no idea precisely what would happen each day in class. And yet, the red flag device quickly created a better learning experience for everyone. In one case, it allowed a very thoughtful and quiet student from India to challenge Anita Roddick on the Body Shop's manufacturing practices in the Third World. Roddick, a charismatic CEO with ferociously held views, usually dominates any discussion. The red flag forced her to listen to a critic. The spirited interchange between these two passionate and well-informed people produced more learning than anything I could have scripted. Without the red flag, we would have just had another session of "I'm CEO and let me tell you how it is."

In another situation, a student used her red flag to state, "Professor Collins, I think you are doing a particularly ineffective job of running class today. You are leading too much with your questions and stifling our independent thinking. Let us think for ourselves." That was a tough moment for me. My BHAG as a professor was to create the most popular class at the business school while imposing the highest workload and the stiffest daily standards. The red flag system confronted me with the fact that my own questioning style stood in the way of my dream—but it also pointed the way to improvement, again, to everyone's benefit.

Interestingly, no other professors on campus adopted the red flag. One of them told me, "I can't imagine doing that. I mean, you never know what might happen. I could never give up that much control in my classroom." What he and others missed was a great paradox: by giving up control and decreasing predictability, you increase the probability of attaining extraordinary results.

Characteristic 2: A catalytic mechanism distributes power for the benefit of the overall system, often to the great discomfort of those who traditionally hold power

With enough power, executives can always get people to jump through hoops. If it is customer service they are after, for instance, they can threaten dismissal to coerce sales-people to smile and act friendly. If they seek higher profits per store, they can pay employees according to flowthrough. And if increased market share is the dream, they can promote only those managers who make it happen.

But consider how catalytic mechanisms work. Short pay distributes power to the customer, to the great discomfort of Granite Rock's executives, but toward the greater goal of continuous improvement for the benefit of customers and company alike. The red flag distributes power to the students, to the great discomfort of the teacher, but to the ultimate improvement of learning in general. The founders of the United States

understood this point when they wrote the
Constitution. After all, the Constitution is
the set of catalytic mechanisms that reinforce
and support the national vision. Voting,
the system of checks and balances, the two-
thirds vote to amend, the impeachment
process—these disperse power away from
one central source, to the great discomfort of
those who seek power, but to the benefit of
the overall nation.

Catalytic mechanisms force the right things
to happen even though those in power often
have a vested interest in the right things *not*
happening. Or they have a vested interest in
inertia—letting pointless, expensive practices stay in place. That's what happened for
years, perhaps decades, at U.S. Marine recruit

depots. All recruits are issued a uniform on
their first day. Two weeks later, they need
another—the pounds melt away when you
run 12 miles every dawn. The military's rules
required those two-week-old uniforms to
be destroyed. Not washed and reissued, but
destroyed.

In the early 1990s, Phil Archuleta, a
materials manager at a recruiting depot
in San Diego, suggested that they reuse
the uniforms. His boss's response: "No.
It's against regulations. Forget about it."
So in a fabulous act of insubordination,
Archuleta washed the uniforms, hid them
in boxes, and bided his time until he finally
got a supervisor willing to challenge the
regulation.

In an effort to empower the Phil Archuletas of the world, the government launched a wide-ranging initiative in 1994 to fix its bureaucratic quagmire. A new rule regarding waivers was put in place, and it is a catalytic mechanism that exemplifies the beauty and power of redistributing power. It has two primary components:

- Waiver-of-regulation requests must be acted upon within 30 days. After 30 days, if no answer is forthcoming, the party asking for the waiver can *assume approval* and implement the waiver.

- Those officials who have the authority to change regulations can approve waiver requests, but *only the head of an agency* can deny a request.

Think for a minute about the impact of this catalytic mechanism. It subverts the default, knee-jerk tendency of bureaucracies to choose inaction over action, status quo over change, and idiotic rules over common sense. Supervisors can no longer say no or not respond. They would have to champion a no all the way to the head of their agency— the equivalent of the head commandant of the entire U.S. Marine Corps—within 30 days. Instead of having to go out of their way to demonstrate why it is a good idea, they would have to expend great energy to prove that it is a *bad* idea. The catalytic mechanism tilts the balance of power away from inertia and toward change.

Indeed, the primary effect of the new waiver rule—as with all catalytic mechanisms—is to give people the freedom to do the right thing. The waiver that allowed Archuleta to change the regulation on uni- forms created a savings of half a million dollars in two years. Similar examples of people doing the right thing with the waiver rule abound throughout the federal govern- ment, from the FDA to NASA. Tort claims adjusters in the Department of Agriculture, for instance, waived regulations to reduce processing time of claims from 51 days to eight days—a manpower savings of 84%. When executives vest people with power and responsibility and step out of the way, vast reservoirs of energy and competence flow forth. Again we have a paradox: the more executives disperse power and responsibility, the more likely the organization is to reach its big, hairy, audacious goal.

Characteristic 3: A catalytic mechanism has teeth

Lots of companies dream of total customer satisfaction; few have a device for making it happen that has the teeth of short pay. Plenty of organizations state the lofty intention to empower people; few translate that into results with a mechanism that has the teeth of the red flag. Many companies state that they intend to "become number one or number two in every competitive arena"; few have added an effective means of enforcement by saying, "and if the business is not number one or number two, or on a clear trajectory to get there, *we will exit within three months.*"

The fact is, executives spend hours drafting, redrafting, and redrafting yet again statements of core values, missions, and visions. This is often a very useful process, but a statement by itself will not accomplish anything. By contrast, a catalytic mechanism puts a process in place that all but guarantees that the vision will be fulfilled. A catalytic mechanism has a sharp set of teeth.

Consider the case of Nucor Corporation, the most successful U.S. steel company of

the last three decades. It has a unique vision
for a Rust Belt company: to be an organization whose workers and management share
the common goal of being the most efficient,
high-quality steel operation in the world,
thereby creating job security and corporate
prosperity in an industry ravaged by foreign
competition. Behind that vision lies the
belief held deeply by Nucor's senior leaders
that decent, hard-working people should
be well paid for their efforts and, so long as
they are highly productive, that they need
not worry about job security. On the surface,
Nucor's vision may sound warm and fuzzy.
Dig deeper, and you'll see that it actually
leaves no room for unproductive employees. Nucor has created a culture of intense

productivity whereby five people do the work that ten do at other steel companies, and get paid like eight. The vision came to life through a series of powerful catalytic mechanisms with teeth, such as the way frontline workers get paid:

- Base hourly pay is 25% to 33% below the industry average.

- People work in teams of 20 to 40; team-productivity rankings are posted daily.

- A bonus of 80% to 200% of base pay, based on *team* productivity, is paid weekly to all teams that meet or exceed productivity goals.

- If you are five minutes late, you lose your bonus for the day.

- If you are 30 minutes late, you lose your bonus for the week.

- If a machine breaks down, thereby stopping production, there is no compensating adjustment in the bonus calculation.

- If a product is returned for poor quality, bonus pay declines accordingly.

You might be thinking that the Nucor system concentrates power in the hands of management, which would seem to contradict the idea of distributing power for the sake of the system. But in fact, the catalytic mechanism actually takes the power out of the hands of individual managers and their whims. Nucor has no discretionary bonuses. It's more like a sports bonus system: if you score so many points or win a certain number of races, you get a bonus based on a predetermined formula. Period. That formula gives workers more power over their own destiny than bonus programs that give large discretionary power to management. If your team scores the points, your team gets the bonus, and no manager can take it away, citing, "We're just not having a very good year" or "I don't like your attitude."

Nucor's catalytic mechanisms for managers, incidentally, have even sharper teeth. Its executive compensation system works very much like its worker compensation system, except that the "team" is the entire plant (for plant managers) or the entire company (for corporate officers). And, unlike most companies, when times are bad, Nucor's executives assume greater pain than front-line workers: workers' pay drops about 25%, plant managers' pay drops about 40%, and corporate officers' pay drops about 60%. In the 1982 recession, CEO Ken Iverson's pay dropped 75%.

Characteristic 4: A catalytic mechanism ejects viruses

A lot of traditional controls are designed to get employees to act the "right" way and do the "right" things, even if they are not so inclined. Catalytic mechanisms, by contrast, help organizations to get the right people in the first place, keep them, and eject those who do not share the company's core values.

Great organizations have figured something out. The old adage "People are your most important asset" is wrong; the *right* people are your most important asset. The right people are those who would exhibit the desired behaviors anyway, as a natural extension of their character and attitude, regardless of any control and incentive system. The challenge is not to train all people to share your core values. The real challenge is to find people who already share your core values and to create catalytic mechanisms that so strongly reinforce those values that the people who don't share them either never get hired or, if they do, they self-eject.

Let's return to the Nucor example. Nucor doesn't try to make lazy people productive. Its catalytic mechanisms create a high-performance environment in which those with an innate work ethic thrive and free riders get out in a hurry. Management usually doesn't fire unproductive workers; *workers* do. In one case, team members chased a lazy coworker out of the plant. And one reporter writing a story on Nucor described showing up for a shift on time but thinking he was late because all the workers had been there for 30 minutes arranging their tools and getting ready to fire off the starting line precisely at 7:00 a.m.

Interestingly, Nucor sets up its mills not in traditional steel towns, but primarily in rural, agricultural areas. The thinking is simple: you can't teach the work ethic—either a person has it or he doesn't. But you can teach steel making. That's why Nucor hires farmers and trains them. The company's catalytic mechanisms wouldn't have it any other way.

Another example of a catalytic mechanism ejecting viruses comes from W.L. Gore & Associates, a fabric company worth nearly $2 billion. Bill Gore founded the company in 1958 with the vision of creating a culture of natural leadership. Leadership, in Gore's view, could not be assigned or bestowed by hierarchical position. You are a leader if and only if people choose to follow you. Gore's theory sprang not just from his personal values but also from his business sense: he thought that the most creative and productive work came when people freely made commitments to one another, not when bosses told them what to do.

To turn his vision into reality, Gore invented a catalytic mechanism that attracted the right people like a magnet and scared away the others. At W.L. Gore & Associates, employees have the authority to fire their bosses. Now, they can't fire the person from the company but, if they feel their boss isn't leading them effectively, they can simply bypass him or her and follow a different leader.

Who would want to work at such a company? Exactly the people who belong there—people who know they can lead without the crutch of a formal position or title and who believe in the philosophy of nonhierarchical leadership. Who would avoid it like the plague? Anyone who gets giddy pulling the levers of position and power just for the pulling's sake. And if you're a hierarchical leader who happens to make it through the company's door but can't quickly shake the notion that "the boss has to be the boss," it won't take you long to find the exit.

Characteristic 5: A catalytic mechanism produces an ongoing effect

Catalytic mechanisms differ fundamentally from catalytic events. A rousing speech to the troops, an electrifying off-site meeting, a euphoria-producing new buzzword, a new initiative or strategic imperative, an impending crisis—all of these are catalytic events, and some are useful. But they do not produce the persistent, ongoing effect of catalytic mechanisms. In fact, a good catalytic mechanism, as long as it evolves, can last for decades, as the 15% rule at 3M and the impeachment mechanism in the Constitution illustrate.

The lack of catalytic mechanisms is one reason many organizations rally in a crisis but languish once the crisis has passed. Leaders who feign a crisis—those who create a burning platform without simultaneously building catalytic mechanisms—do more long-term harm than good by creating a syndrome of crisis addiction. Executives who rely only on catalytic events are left wondering why the momentum stalls after the first phase of euphoria, excitement, or fear has passed. To produce lasting results, they must shift from orchestrating a series of events to building catalytic mechanisms.

Take, for example, the decades of ineffectual attempts to reform public education in the United States. Part of the failure lies in the approach to reform; too often it is based on onetime events and fashionable buzzwords rather than on catalytic mechanisms that produce sustained effects. As Roger Briggs, a high school teacher in Boulder, Colorado, wrote in an essay on school reform: "Every year we get a new program or fad. And they never really work. And we teachers eventually just learn to ignore them, smile, and go about our business of teaching." Now take a look at what happened when the state of Texas started using a catalytic mechanism in 1995: comparison-band ranking of schools, which is directly tied to resource allocation and, in some cases, school closures. The ongoing effect of this device forced the momentum of reform forward. Why? Well, if you rank fifth out of 40 schools but you just sit still, you'll drop in the ratings. Sit still long enough, and you'll eventually rank 35th rather than fifth, and you may face closure. Because every school is ranked on the same criteria, the bar for performance keeps rising. Within four years of installing the mechanism, student achievement in Texas improved across the board. The percentage of students who passed the Texas math skill exam, for example, rose from roughly half to 80%, and the share of black and Hispanic students who passed doubled to 64% and 72%, respectively.

And consider the ongoing impact of a good catalytic mechanism in a more corporate setting. Darwin Smith, former CEO of Kimberly-Clark, created in 1971 the BHAG to transform Kimberly-Clark from a mediocre forest- and paper-products company into a world-class consumer goods company. At the time, Wall Street analysts scoffed at the idea, as did most of Kimberly-Clark's competitors. Smith was undeterred. He created one catalytic event and one equally important catalytic mechanism. For the first, he sold a big chunk of the company's traditional paper-production mills, thus leaving no easy escape route from the dream. For the second, he committed the company to head-to-head competition with the best consumer-products company in the world: Procter & Gamble. With its entry into disposable diapers, Kimberly-Clark would henceforth be a direct rival of P&G. Kimberly-Clark would either become excellent at consumer products or get crushed. The beauty of this catalytic mechanism is that, unlike the "change or die" ranting all too common among modern executives, its ongoing effect is as powerful today as when it was first put in place nearly 30 years ago.

GETTING STARTED

This is not intended to be a how-to article; my main objective has been to introduce the concept of catalytic mechanisms and demonstrate how they have helped some companies—and individuals—turn their BHAGs into reality. (For more on the personal use of catalytic mechanisms, see the insert "Not for Companies Only.") Nonetheless, my research suggests that there are a few general principles that support the process of building catalytic mechanisms effectively.

Don't just add, remove

When pursuing BHAGs, our natural inclination is to add—new initiatives, new systems, new strategies, new priorities, and now, new catalytic mechanisms. But in doing so, we overwhelm ourselves. Isn't it frightening that the new version of the Palm Pilot has space for 1,500 items on its to-do list? Sadly, few of us have a "stop doing" list. We should, because to take something away—to unplug it—can be as catalytic as adding something new.

Take the case of a circuit division at Hewlett-Packard. It had tried countless programs and initiatives to reach its BHAG of becoming "a place where people would walk on the balls of their feet, feel exhilarated about their work, and search for imaginative ways to improve and innovate everything we do." The events produced short-term results—a moment of sparkle and excitement—but within a month or two, the division always drifted back into its sleepy, humdrum mode.

Then its executives considered the question, "What policies should we remove?" For most of its history, the division had comfortably lived off a captive internal market. What if HP's divisions were allowed to buy their components from outside competitors? Never again would the circuit division have fat internal orders just handed to it. Never again could it just sit still. Two months, four months, a year, five years, and ten years down the road—fierce competitors would still be there, constantly upping the ante. The prospect was both terrifying and exhilarating. Managers decided to unplug the "buy internal" requirement and open the doors to free-market competition.

Within weeks, the circuit division was well on its way to realizing its BHAG. You could sense a completely different environment the moment you walked in the door. The place hummed with activity, and its performance showed it.

Create, don't copy

Creating mechanisms is exactly that: a creative act. You can, of course, get good ideas by looking at what other organizations do, but the best catalytic mechanisms are idiosyncratic adaptations, if not wholesale creations, for a unique situation.

Because catalytic mechanisms require fresh ideas, it makes sense to invite all members of an organization to participate in their creation. Everyone. Certainly, some mechanisms require input from senior executives, like short pay at Granite Rock. Yet many of the best catalytic mechanisms were not created by top management. The idea for the federal government's waiver rule, for example, originated with two staff members—Lance Cope and Jeff Goldstein. They were working in the national reinvention labs, and neither had direct authority over any federal agency.

Allow me also to use a personal example. Part of my professional vision is to contribute through teaching and to harness my curiosity and passion for learning in ways that make a positive impact on the world. From that goal flows the imperative that I allocate time primarily to research, writing, and teaching and limit consulting work only to those situations in which I can contribute as a teacher.

To reinforce that imperative, I have created two catalytic mechanisms: the "come to Boulder rule" and the "four day rule." The first rule states that I will not engage in a direct advisory relationship with any organization unless the chief executive agrees to travel to my Boulder research laboratory. Executives spend huge sums of money on consultants, but money doesn't equal commitment—if you have a big enough budget, invoices just don't hurt. Yet all chief executives, no matter how large their budgets, have only 24 hours in a day. If a CEO flies all the way to Boulder, he or she has demonstrated commitment to serious discussions and hard work, and the likelihood that I will make a significant impact as a teacher increases exponentially. Most important, those not committed to real (and perhaps uncomfortable) change eject right up front.

The second mechanism—my four-day rule—states that any given organization has an upper limit of four days of my advisory time in a year. The most lasting impact comes by teaching people how to fish, not by fishing for them. Organizations that want an adviser to fish for them self-eject through this catalytic mechanism. Admittedly, these are highly unusual devices, and they would be disastrous for most consulting firms that depend on continuous growth to feed their machine. Yet they are perfectly designed for a strategy aimed at explicitly *not* building a large consulting business. They are unique to me, as all catalytic mechanisms should be to their creators.

Use money, but not only money

The examples in this article may lead you to believe that most catalytic mechanisms use money. But, in fact, when my research colleague Lane Hornung cataloged my database of catalytic mechanisms, he found that only half do. That might surprise some people—in particular those who ascribe to the old saw that money is the best motivator. I'm not going to claim that money doesn't impel people toward desired results; money can add teeth to any catalytic mechanism. But to rely entirely on money reflects a shallow understanding of human behavior.

The U.S. Marine Corps illustrates my point precisely. The Corps builds extraordinary commitment through a set of catalytic mechanisms that create intense psychological bonds among its members. By isolating recruits at boot camps and creating an environment where recruits survive only by relying upon one another, the Corps triggers the deep human drive, hardwired into most of us, to support and protect those we consider family. Most people will not risk their lives for a year-end bonus, but they will go to great lengths to earn the respect and protect the well-being of their comrades.

William Manchester, who returned to his unit on Okinawa after receiving a wound that earned him a Purple Heart, eloquently describes the psychology of commitment in his book *Goodbye Darkness*:

And then, in one of those great thundering jolts in which a man's real motives are revealed to him in an electrifying vision, I understand, at last, why I jumped hospital that Sunday thirty-five years ago, and, in violation of orders, returned to the front and almost certain death. It was an act of love. Those men on the line were my family, my home. . . . They had never let me down, and I couldn't do it to them. I had to be with them rather than to let them die and me live with the knowledge that I might have saved them. Men, I now knew, do not fight for flag or country, for the Marine Corps or glory or any other abstraction. They fight for one another.[1]

Yes, catalytic mechanisms sometimes use money to add bite, but the best ones also tap deeper wells of human motivation. Even at Nucor, the effectiveness of its catalytic mechanisms lies as much in the peer pressure and the desire to not let teammates down as in the number of dollars in the weekly bonus envelope. The best people *never* work solely for money. And catalytic mechanisms should reflect that fact.

Allow your mechanisms to evolve

New catalytic mechanisms sometimes produce unintended negative consequences and need correction. For instance, the first version of the red flag failed because certain students continued to dominate class discussion, thinking that every comment of theirs was worth a red flag. So I added the stipulation: "Your red flag can be used only once during the quarter. Your red flag is nontransferable; you cannot give or sell it to another student."

All catalytic mechanisms, in fact, even if they work perfectly at first, should evolve. 3M's 15% rule is a case in point. In 1956, executives urged 3M scientists to use 3M labs during their lunch break to work on anything they wanted. In the 1960s, that catalytic mechanism became formalized as the "15% rule," whereby scientists could use *any* 15% of their time. In the 1980s, the 15% rule became widely available to 3Mers other than scientists, to be used for manufacturing and marketing innovations, for example. In the 1990s, 3M's executives worried that fewer people were using the mechanism than in previous decades. It put together a task force to reinvent the 15% rule, bolstering it with special recognition rewards for those who used their "bootleg time"—as it has come to be called—to create profitable innovations.

The 15% rule has been a catalytic mechanism at 3M for more than 40 years, but it has continually evolved in order to remain relevant and effective. That's the right approach; no catalytic mechanism should be viewed as sacred. In a great company, only the core values and purpose are sacred; everything else, including a catalytic mechanism, should be open for change.

Build an integrated set

One catalytic mechanism is good; several that reinforce one another as a set is even better. That's not to say a company needs hundreds of catalytic mechanisms—a handful

will do. Consider Granite Rock again. It
certainly doesn't rely just on short pay. It
also has a catalytic mechanism that requires
an employee and manager to create a
focused development plan for the employee
during the performance evaluation process.
Indeed, every employee and manager must
together complete a form that reads: "Learn
_____ so that I can contribute _____."
Two sets of teeth make this form effective.
First, employees and their managers must
both sign off on the final development plan,
which forces a continual dialogue until they
reach agreement. Second, compensation
ties directly to learning and improvement,
not just job performance: people who do not
go out of their way to improve their skills

receive lower than midpoint pay. Only those who do a good job *and* improve their skills *and* make a contribution to improving the overall Granite Rock system receive higher than midpoint pay. So people who merely do a good job self-eject out of Granite Rock. This catalytic mechanism has produced delightful surprises: one previously illiterate employee used it to get the company to send him to a reading program. When Granite Rock won the Baldrige Award, he read an acceptance speech.

Granite Rock also uses catalytic mechanisms to guide hiring, encourage risk taking, and stimulate new capabilities. The point here is not so much in the details as it is in the big picture: Granite Rock does not rely solely on short pay to pursue its BHAG of attaining a reputation for customer satisfaction that exceeds Nordstrom's. It has about a dozen catalytic mechanisms that support and reinforce one another.

That said, however, it would be a mistake to take this article and launch a grand catalytic mechanism initiative. Developing a set of catalytic mechanisms should be an organic process, an ongoing discipline, a habit of mind and action. The dozen or so catalytic mechanisms at Granite Rock came into being over a ten-year period. You certainly don't want to use the idea to create another layer of bureaucracy. Catalytic mechanisms should be catalysts, not inhibitors.

CASTLES IN THE AIR

I recently worked with a large retail chain to define its BHAG for the twenty-first century. The company is doing well, but it wants its performance to be outrageously great. And so its executives came up with a wildly ambitious goal: to make its brand more popular than Coke.

That company's challenge now is to invent the catalytic mechanisms that will make the dream a reality. I've advised its executives against investing heavily in hoopla events to fire up thousands of frontline employees about the new BHAG. Instead, they should create and implement a set of catalytic mechanisms—specific, concrete, and powerful devices to lend discipline to their vision.

After all, catalytic mechanisms alone will not create greatness; they need a dream to guide them. But if you can blend huge, intangible aspirations with simple, tangible catalytic mechanisms, then you'll have the magic combination from which sustained excellence grows.

At the conclusion of *Walden,* Henry David Thoreau wrote: "If you have built castles in the air, your work need not be lost; that is where they should be. Now put the foundations under them." BHAGs are a company's wildest dreams. Catalytic mechanisms are their foundations. Build them both.

TABLE 1

Catalytic mechanisms: Breaking from tradition

Catalytic mechanisms share five distinct characteristics that distinguish them from traditional controls

A traditional managerial device, control, or mechanism:	A catalytic mechanism:	Examples of catalytic mechanisms:
Reduces variation as it enlarges the organization's bureaucracy.	Produces desired results in unpredictable ways.	The red flag made a ferociously opinionated CEO listen to the challenge of an M.B.A. student—improving the knowledge of the whole class, despite the unexpected nature of the exchange.
Concentrates power in the hands of authorities who can force people to obey their commands.	Distributes power for the benefit of the overall system, often to the great discomfort of those who traditionally hold power.	A new government rule allowed a low-level manager to expunge an immensely wasteful regulation that required nearly new uniforms to be burned.

(Continued)

TABLE 1 (CONTINUED)

A traditional managerial device, control, or mechanism:	A catalytic mechanism:	Examples of catalytic mechanisms:
Is understood by employees and executives alike as merely an intention.	Has a sharp set of teeth.	Short pay at Granite Rock allows customers to pay only for the products that satisfy them.
Attempts to stimulate the right behaviors from the wrong people.	Attracts the right people and ejects viruses.	At W.L. Gore & Associates, employees can, in effect, fire their bosses, ensuring nonhierarchical leadership.
Has the short-lived impact of a single event or a fad.	Produces an ongoing effect.	Kimberly-Clark knowingly put itself into head-to-head competition with Procter & Gamble to impel better performance in the consumer goods marketplace. Such a strategy is still working 30 years later.

Anatomy of a BHAG

In our research for *Built to Last,* Jerry Porras
and I discovered that most enduring great
companies set and pursue BHAGs (pro-
nounced BEE-hags and shorthand for big,
hairy, audacious goals). There are three key
characteristics of a good BHAG:

1. **It has a long time frame—ten to 30
   years or more.** The whole point of a
   BHAG is to stimulate your organization to
   make changes that dramatically improve
   its fundamental capabilities over the long
   run. Citicorp's first BHAG, set in 1915—
   to become the most powerful, the most
   serviceable, the most far-reaching world
   financial institution ever—took more than

five decades to achieve. Its new BHAG, set in the early 1990s—to attain 1 billion customers worldwide—will require at least two decades to achieve. (Today it has less than 100 million.) BHAGs with short time frames can lead executives to sacrifice long-term results for the sake of achieving a short-term goal.

2. **It is clear, compelling, and easy to grasp.** The goal in a good BHAG is obvious, no matter how you phrase it. For example, Philip Morris's BHAG, set in the 1950s—to knock off R.J. Reynolds as the number one tobacco company in the world—didn't leave much room for confusion. I call this the "Mount Everest

standard." The goal to climb Mount
Everest can be said as "Climb the most
famous mountain in the world" or "Climb
the biggest mountain in the world" or
"Climb the mountain at 87 degrees east,
28 degrees north" or "Climb the mountain
in Nepal that measures 29,028 feet" or
hundreds of other ways. If you find yourself
spending countless hours tinkering with a
statement, you don't yet have a BHAG.

3. **It connects to the core values and
   purpose of the organization.** The best
   BHAGs aren't random; they fit with the
   fundamental core values and reason
   for being of the company. For example,
   Nike's BHAG in the 1960s—to crush

Adidas—fit perfectly with Nike's core purpose "to experience the emotion of competition, winning, and crushing competitors." Sony's BHAG in the 1950s—to become the company most known for changing the worldwide poor-quality image of Japanese products—flowed directly from its stated core value of elevating the Japanese culture and national status.

This last criterion connects back to the reason for having a BHAG in the first place. It is a powerful way to stimulate progress—change, improvement, innovation, renewal—while simultaneously preserving your core values and purpose. It is this remarkable ability to blend continuity with change that separates

enduring great companies from merely successful ones. The trick, of course, is not just to
set a BHAG but to achieve it, and therein lies
the power of catalytic mechanisms.

Not for Companies Only

My research has focused on the impact
of catalytic mechanisms in organizational
settings—on how they can turn a company's
most ambitious goals into reality. But catalytic
mechanisms can also have a powerful impact
on individuals. Indeed, I have made catalytic
mechanisms a fundamental part of how I man-
age my time, with my "come to Boulder rule"
and "four day rule."

I am not alone. Several of my former students at Stanford Business School have applied a catalytic mechanism to reach their goals. In one case, a student emerged from his courses on entrepreneurship fired up by the idea of forgoing the traditional path and striking out on his own. But as time passed and he felt the crushing burden of school debt as well as the lure of lucrative job offers, his personal vision waned. He took a job at a large, established disc drive manufacturer and promised himself, "I'm going to launch out on my own in five years when I've paid off all my school debts."

In most cases, such dreams fade as the years go by—with the advent of cars, houses, children, and all the rest. My former student,

however, implemented an interesting catalytic mechanism to keep his vision alive. He
drafted a resignation letter and dated it five
years out. Then he gave copies of the letter
to a handful of reliable people, along with the
following instructions, "If I don't leave my job
and launch out on my own by the specified
date, then send the letter in for me." His plan
worked. In 1996, I received an e-mail from him
that described how he saved his money and
spent his off-hours developing his entrepre-
neurial options. Then, right on schedule, he
quit his secure job and launched a fund to buy
and run his own company.

In another case, a former student created
a personal board of directors composed of
people he admires and would not want to

Jim Collins

disappoint, and he made a personal commitment to follow the board's guidance—it
has power in his life. In 1996, he wrote me:
"I recently used my personal board in decid-
ing whether to leave Morgan Stanley and
go to work with a friend in his two-year-old
business. 'Yes' was the unanimous vote."
So despite the risk of leaving a lucrative and
prestigious position, he leapt into the small
company, which has since grown fourfold to
employ more than 80 people.

Consider also the highly effective catalytic
mechanism that a colleague of mine has
been using for the past three years to attain
her BHAG: to lead a full and active life as a
mother, wife, professional writer, and church
volunteer, without going crazy. That part

{ 70 }

about maintaining sanity is important because before her catalytic mechanism was in place, my colleague constantly found herself overextended and miserable. The main culprit was her work as a freelance writer: she accepted too many jobs. "Even if we didn't need the money, I would still take on every project that came my way," she recalls. "Maybe because my family was so poor when I was growing up, I just found it impossible to leave money on the table." Not surprisingly, the woman's children paid the price of her constant working, as did her husband and close-knit extended family. "Either I was too exhausted to see people or else I was calling them for a baby-sitting favor," she says.

One day, my colleague was lamenting her situation to her sister, who came up with an effective catalytic mechanism. Every time the woman took on work beyond a certain level of revenue—a comfortable annual salary, in essence—she would pay her sister a $200-a-day penalty fee. My colleague, instantly seeing the wonderful impact of the plan, immediately agreed.

Since she redistributed power to her sister, my colleague has gained new control over her life. Now she happily accepts jobs up to a certain level of income, but she assesses each additional offer with newly critical eyes. (She has taken on extra work on only two occasions; both projects were too lucrative to pass up.) Indeed, the catalytic mechanism has so freed my colleague from overwork that she has taken on a new role as a volunteer at her children's school. With its undeniable bite, my colleague's catalytic mechanism will have an ongoing effect as long as she honors it. And given its results, she plans to do so for a long time.

Would any of these people have changed their lives without catalytic mechanisms? Perhaps, but I think it less likely. Personal catalytic mechanisms have all the benefits of organizational mechanisms: they put bite into good intentions, dramatically increasing the odds of actually being true to your personal vision instead of letting your dreams remain unrealized.

NOTE

1. William Manchester, *Goodbye Darkness* (Boston: Little, Brown and Company, 1979).

ABOUT THE AUTHOR

Jim Collins operates a management research laboratory in Boulder, Colorado. He is the coauthor, with Jerry I. Porras, of *Built to Last: Successful Habits of Visionary Companies* (HarperBusiness, 1994) and of "Building Your Company's Vision" (*HBR* September–October 1996).

Article Summary

Idea in Brief

Many change programs trumpet their arrival with well-known Big Hairy Audacious Goals (BHAGs). But just as many get stuck at the first hurdle to meeting those goals—mobilizing the organization away from the status quo. Catalytic mechanisms help catapult organizations over this hurdle. This simple yet powerful tool enables companies to propel commitment levels past the point of no return. They are galvanizing, nonbureaucratic means of turning visions into reality, usually involving a redistribution of power. Short pay is a defining example of a catalytic mechanism. Granite Rock mobilized its employees to feverish levels of performance improvement with this simple but radical policy that invites customers who are not completely satisfied to reduce their invoice payment—without returning product. Of course, short pay is not appropriate for every company, but other catalytic mechanisms wielding that much power definitely are.

The most important management ideas all in one place.

We hope you enjoyed this book from *Harvard Business Review*. For the best ideas HBR has to offer turn to HBR's 10 Must Reads Boxed Set. From books on leadership and strategy to managing yourself and others, this 6-book collection delivers articles on the most essential business topics to help you succeed.

HBR's 10 Must Reads Series

The definitive collection of ideas and best practices on our most sought-after topics from the best minds in business.

- Change Management
- Collaboration
- Communication
- Emotional Intelligence
- Innovation
- Leadership
- Making Smart Decisions

- Managing Across Cultures
- Managing People
- Managing Yourself
- Strategic Marketing
- Strategy
- Teams
- The Essentials

hbr.org/mustreads

Buy for your team, clients, or event.
Visit hbr.org/bulksales for quantity discount rates.